The Rhizome Hive

Thoughts from the Forest

TOFU INK ARTS PRESS PRESENTS

Mr. Jeff Kass' Creative Writing Prose and Poetry II

TOFU INK ARTS PRESS PRESENTS:
Pioneer High School
Mr. Jeff Kass' Creative Writing Prose and Poetry II
The Rhizome Hive: Thoughts from the Forest
Copyright © 2026 Brian L. Jacobs PhD, MFA
Published by Tofu Ink Arts Press. All rights reserved.
Book design by
Brian L. Jacobs, Jeff Kass, Rashed & JLTY Atelier
Cover Images: Abigail Frankfurt
ISBN: 978-1-958661-38-3
tofuink.com
A member of CLMP

DEDICATED TO

THE A2 HOMETOWN FAV MR. JEFF KASS
AND HIS REMARKABLE STUDENT WRITERS

HAPPY RETIREMENT MR. KASS!

Contents

I can't tell you how much I've enjoyed working with y'all this year.
There is so much talent in this class and when you push yourselves
you're capable of becoming really powerful.
Keep reading. Keep writing. Be kind to each other.
Don't give in to the AI temptation.
When you create, you can be great.
It's been a true privilege to hear your work.
Thank you for being courageous enough to be vulnerable.
Remember one last thing
- adverbs are not your friends.

- Jeff Kass

Creative Writing II is a class where we push students to continue to develop their voices in poetry and prose. We experiment with Formal Verse Fridays and Free Write Fridays and endeavor to introduce students numerous contemporary writers of distinction. The goal is always to help students rediscover a vibrant sense of imagination and to inculcate a belief that their own stories are powerful and important. *Mr. Kass*

The Rhizome Hive: Thoughts from the Forest is about a rhizomatic moment against hegemony and dominance in the year 2026, where creativity is squashed by NO ONE, and where students are rising up with their voices to be heard.

On this one day, students absorbed the possibilities of errantry on a journey to possibilities. Therefore this book.

This book is an emblem of a moment when Brian L. Jacobs came to encounter the brilliance in Mr. Kass' class; where the students made us notice their poetic blast into the abstract of the rhizome (for no good reason) and to show us what can become of becomings.

* * *

A **rhizome** is a modified, thickened underground plant stem that grows horizontally, acting as a primary storage organ for nutrients and water while enabling vegetative propagation in any direction. They possess nodes that produce new roots and shoots, allowing plants to spread and survive unfavorable seasons.

Rhizomatic Poetics is an exciting, creative literary declaration and practice that rejects the hegemonic (dominating) hierarchical roots of traditional thought inspired by the philosophies of Gilles Deleuze and Félix Guattari with Édouard Glissant.

Rhizomatic thinking establishes a non-linear, non-hierarchical mode of creative inquiry for liberation purposes. It moves from the "solid thought" of the root to the "constellation of nodes" of the rhizome, where identity is a fluid network of relations extending outward. ~ Brian L. Jacobs PhD, MFA

Kraken

Angel Luna Dominguez

My heart beats like the sea, full of coral and plastic.
a looming danger like a kraken,
The companies acting like sheep when they're really a wolf
trying to get money out of "saving the ocean."
My feet becoming like the sea, full of coral and life.
like antelopes running from lions who are being hunted by
hunger.
Green all around me even in class like man among nature.

Somewhere Between

Eden Yarmoluk

somewhere between
a thought
and a memory

i lost the point—
and kept going

words drift,
change direction,
don't come back

you don't need
to understand me

i'm not a straight line,
just a series of almosts

Poison is the Cure

Dylan Moore

The tornado in the street shrieks like a broken vacuum.

It spins like a ballet dancer who just won't stop. It breaks apart a house like a paper shredder.

It won't stop until god cuts it like a knife, and it collapses into puddles.

Puddles that the trees soak up.

The tree grows exponentially and spawns apples and oranges on the branches.

Monkeys take juicy bites out of the fruit and throw the uneaten parts on the ground.

Maggots finish the rest.

I watch as they suck the color out of the world.

The plants that keep me alive make me itchy.

I scratch until I'm sore, like my muscles when I improve my strength.

Round and Running

Jillian Cundiff

like a carousel
spinning
round and round,
round
and
run

leave, escape
run
blinding light
bright yellow blinding light
into light
leap
jump
run
walk
crawl
into escape

into childhood
before the death
the silver
on stone
cold hard stone
break

Octopus Thing

Ahmed Faddah

Purple things
around a person
tatted up
all around
Nature
Flowers blooming

Blaine

Donte Bailey

big red colors
run through this Art
inside a squid
turns a mushroom
of nature

Rise of the Beans

Abigail Kilcline

The beans will win
The world will burn
You can scream and cry but there's no beating the devil
We're all going to die
Die we want to die
Dying makes it stop
Stop the world won't end
Peace and maybe then I'll be happy
Happy doesn't exist it's an idea not everyone is meant to be happy
Happiness is scam.
Make it stop.

Crowded With Nobody

Ali Al-Shakdary

When so far ahead of everyone
Theres nothing besides an empty car
Theres no one beside you
and the view from there is the same as
a person from last place

Outsides

Hana Boggess

Meandering sidewalks coarsen grains of sand,
the sun burning, fire lit trees. Water, no fishing.
The oceans salt, and pepper graced pizza
bedazzled sparkles glinting in the eye of a baby,
brown eyed deer gazing into the fountains
spray-stark in paint splatters freedom. A clock winding
in black and white panda print peanut butter puffs, ticking.
White milk, sloshing blocks and chirping of chickadees
in summer's long grueling day and a quench in my bones.

Little Frenetic Mouse

Addison Jackson

So was the chuffed mouse.
Squeaking in a fantod while the breeze above
laughed facinorously at it's schadenfreude.
Gathered pebbles and twigs to witness their irate oust.
"Halt your whips!"
Mouse declared, then poised their little claws.
"For I am ambiogenesis. You may crackle and be so barmy
but I will always be despondent to you!"
Rushing and puffing their chest
like a worked up tomato.
Up into the sky from a farouche gust.
There mouse faced the sun in its siesta,
a blob of harshness to life giving below.
Sunburnt in trepidation.
Understanding all and nothing ever present
to their ribbony whiskers.
Mouse ever so zany, ever so zealous.
Now so abapical.
So was the salient Mouse.

Morning Air Breathes Marrow

Arianna Lehnert

Breath evaporates the sky
Makes it lavender purple
Wait I have to write!
Danger seeps through my marrow
Run away
Snow leopard tracks the mushrooms
Need to focus
The bonsai tree spreads rhizomatically
I breath rhizomatically
grey girl with tentacles
spreads her wings

Idk man 👍

Wyatt Roebuck

I think our government right now is kinda sh*t,
eating kids, and assaulting them,
allowing for the murder of their own civilians by their agencies.
I think it's high time we brought them back down to our level,
show them the reality that they aren't gods
and that they can and will be held responsible,
they have gotten away for far to long.
The more I think
the more I really do wish I could still ask my dad some questions,
like why is it so hard turning into to a man from a boy,
why does it feel like hit after hit every day,
why is it so hard for me just to cry for a few minutes.

The Pyramids of Egypt

Masimba Chikosi

hieroglyphics loquacious
like the dreadlocks of the black man
who wrote them in the sand

sand covering my feet
for i kicked down your sandcastles
and hopped over your walls
intended to keep me and mines out

me and mines making cash in abundance
living a life you and yours could never fathom
me and mines inverting you
and yours reality one hieroglyphic at a time

Qwertyuiopasdfghjklzxcvbnm

Charles Shapiro Bokser

Internal screaming beating my brain
Methylphenidate soothing the cry's
Song of the cleats and soccer balls
My veins blue filled w adrenaline
ADHD meds soothing thoughts
Rush of adrenaline even stronger
Time slows down
Feet move fast
Retinas scanning everything
scanning the face of somone else
Chicken nuggets fill my intestines
White socks black pants white t shirt
Sandwich method with turkey cheese bacon
Chrome hearts beating inside and outside me
Denim tears the clothes I wear
the tears that fall from my eyes
Purified water freezing
Fluctuating thermometer
Every morning Methlyphenidate
White little cylinders
Qwertyuiopasdfghjklzxcvbnm
The jumble of nonsense I see every day

Garnish of Burnt Leaves

Erick Cornell

Songs of sycamore trees
Unheard
Clangs and nangs
Of pots and pans
Sauteed mushrooms
Spores slowly killing a kitchen
Struggles
To get the perfect cook
Always tasting of metal
Reflective
Blinded by iridescent lights
Lights not bound by people
All failing
Lights shatter
All falling
Ashes and rust
In no longer shimmer

Hectic Effervescent Bats

Bella Shemke

Jumping orange mellifluous accordions smack
Small pink bat eat nefarious teeth chomp
Tin foil box-like boxed in
With the cornered paradoxical hoops
Hanging from the polka dot zebra
Green aura that ingests the blue
Overzealous rainbows jump over unicorns
Between the twin cats screaming
Raining sky fly the men
Plastic pigs kill
Without notice from civilians

World Stage

Leium McIntosh

Pierrot stole my face

alcohol swims across black earth

blindness and carnival

music bleeds in a skull, pleasure sings in its chains

tightrope around my neck

sex is good,

a knife f*cks me

masks become a face

baptism in daisies

Tartaglia's words shatter into clouds

the Innamorati slit their throats, bouquets, moonlight

Sandrone freezes, fires of shame

Make me happy

kill yourself

Grazie Mille

Comedia Dell'Arte

The Purple Giraffe.

Fritz Bauer

The Purple Giraffe.

The star crab puts you into a dream.

The Turtles swim through the sky.

The legumes rest within the corner of a bag.

The pyramid of toasters lie.

The banana lays.

The sexy guppy signals.

The giant heart beats.

The gate whispers of money.

I am a Purple Giraffe.

The Vines

Evylynn Clark

can you feel the vines at your ankles?
are they wrapping around a little too tightly
in a way that makes you feel like you cant breathe?
in a way thats a little too itchy or uncomfortable?
have you asked them to stop,
loosen their grip?
no that wouldn't work, would it?
have you grabbed your sheers to cut them loose?
in between your panicked breaths,
have you had the thought,
that the vines didn't know they were bothering you?
that it was an accident?
the vines were not thinking straight.
give the vines some grace
don't blame the vines.
with a mind and thoughts of their very own.
don't blame the vines.

Ulcers Come Aching

Brian L. Jacobs

those who do not know this peppermint set in platinum
must pray to death and beauty that glory and eternity can still toil
the sow'r
the ulcers come aching
and obliterated amongst this sacred geography
this pilgrim
a consultation with dirt
hounded and neglected
in mutants of memory
as ash'd heretics are burned like stick fire on the seared heaps
marking the unremarkable reified in my recenter

Crashing Out

Jeff Kass

On your bike, in your head, in your car
in the kitchen, in the mist, swerve, swerve
swerve, jump around, jump around, get
the fishhooks out the sides of your head
the flounder of your laptop out of your head
your head your head your bouncing ball
head your truck-bed head, your beanpole head
take a tour in your head, crash out, crash out
remember Modern English, the movie Valley
Girl, you watched it in the mall on a date
you didn't kiss, you were too scared,
crash out, crash out, remember
the guy who cut you off then drive
too slow, crash out, crash out, remember
getting kicked out of the party when
you were supposed to be the Dee-Jay
spin the record, crash out, crash out
spin out on your bicycle, shoulder
smacking pavement, cars bending
around you, oh, gymnastics, oh, figure
skating, oh, falling down, Lindsey Vonn
shatter your femur, oh, ski slope, oh,
burning building, crash out, crash out,
oh Popeye overdosed on spinach, oh,
Scooby vomiting up your scooby snacks,
Too much, too much, Instagram stop

Reeling, Tik stop toking, oh, bullfrog,
oh, office politics, oh, Wuthering Heights,
oh, Cowardly Lion, wherefore art thou,
Sandy Koufax? Wherefore art thou,
Johnny Podres, Sophia Loren, Prince
Valiant, flying Orangutan, wherefore
art thou frozen stapler, electric free
fang chicken, wherefore art thou, God-
Mother of the greens, the blues, the purples
And pouches, wherefore art thou, mattress
of the wilderness, master of the childless,
throat coated with strawberry aspirin, foot
coated with bookshelves, showerheads, slack
skin, Rumplestilt bin of storied history, crash
out, hash out, mash the potatoes, slash
the windows, bash the skyscraper, what
is the golden grail, what is the silver pomade,
how clingy is the spaghetti, the risotto, boil
it, spoil it, coil it, roil it, cash it in, crash it
out, smash it out – all the girders crumbling
bumbling, everything stumbling, cash in your
chips, smash all your ships, crash out, crash out
crash into your heart, crash into the spring
of your Achilles tendon, crash out. Crash,
crash, crash out.

www.ingramcontent.com/pod-product-compliance
Lightning Source LLC
Chambersburg PA
CBHW021349060726
47591CB00006B/2239